HAVE FUN READING THIS BOOK!

IT OFFERS SOME REAL SURVIVAL TIPS. BUT THE SETTINGS ARE NOT REAL. THINK ABOUT HOW YOU CAN USE THESE HACKS IN REAL LIFE. USE COMMON SENSE. BE SAFE AND ASK AN ADULT FOR PERMISSION AND HELP WHEN NEEDED.

45th Parallel Press

Published in the United States of America by Cherry Lake Publishing
Ann Arbor, Michigan
www.cherrylakepublishing.com

Reading Adviser: Marla Conn, MS, Ed., Literacy specialist, Read-Ability, Inc.
Book Designer: Felicia Macheske

Photo Credits: © solar22/Shutterstock.com,cover; © FOTOKITA/Shutterstock.com, 5; © Borkin Vadim/
Shutterstock.com, 6; © pathdoc/Shutterstock.com, 9; © Dudarev Mikhail/Shutterstock.com, 11; © Anteromite/
Shutterstock.com, 13; © Mastaco/Shutterstock.com, 14; © Good Luck Photo/Shutterstock.com, 17; © bogdan
ionescu/Shutterstock.com, 19; © Gabriel_Ramos/Shutterstock.com, 21; © photogal/Shutterstock.com, 21;
© Josephine Billeter/Shutterstock.com, 22; © worker/Shutterstock.com, 25; © Tompet/Shutterstock.com, 27
;© aopsan/Shutterstock.com, 29

Graphic Elements Throughout: © SrsPvl Witch/Shutterstock.com; © Igor Vitkovskiy/Shutterstock.com; ©
FabrikaSimf/Shutterstock.com; © bulbspark/Shutterstock.com; © donatas1205/Shutterstock.com; © NinaM/
Shutterstock.com; © Picsfive/Shutterstock.com; © prapann/Shutterstock.com; © S_Kuzmin/Shutterstock.com
© autsawin uttisin/Shutterstock.com; © xpixel/Shutterstock.com; © OoddySmile/Shutterstock.com; © ilikestudio/
Shutterstock.com; © Kues/Shutterstock.com; © ankomando/Shutterstock.com; © Liubou Yasiukovich/
Shutterstock.com; © VectorArtFactory/Shutterstock.com; © Bakai/Shutterstock.com; © popcic/Shutterstock.com;

45th Parallel Press is an imprint of Cherry Lake Publishing.

Library of Congress Cataloging-in-Publication Data

Names: Loh-Hagan, Virginia, author.
Title: Zombie apocalypse hacks / Virginia Loh-Hagan.
Description: Ann Arbor, MI : Cherry Lake Publishing, [2019] | Series: Could
 you survive? | Includes bibliographical
 references and index.
Identifiers: LCCN 2019006169| ISBN 9781534147799 (hardcover) | ISBN
 9781534150652 (pbk.) | ISBN 9781534149229 (pdf) | ISBN 9781534152083
 (hosted ebook)
Subjects: LCSH: Survival—Juvenile literature. | Zombies—Juvenile literature.
Classification: LCC GF86 .L6429 2019 | DDC 613.6/9—dc23
LC record available at https://lccn.loc.gov/2019006169

Cherry Lake Publishing would like to acknowledge the work of The Partnership for 21st Century Skills.
Please visit *www.p21.org* for more information.

Printed in the United States of America
Corporate Graphics

Dr. Virginia Loh-Hagan is an author, university professor, former classroom teacher, and curriculum designer.
A zombie apocalypse scares her. She's out of shape. And she's lazy. She'd get bitten by a zombie. She lives in
San Diego with her very tall husband and very naughty dogs. To learn more about her, visit www.virginialoh.com.

INTRODUCTION 4

CHAPTER 1
PROTECT YOUR BODY! 11

CHAPTER 2
HIDE YOUR SMELL! 15

CHAPTER 3
BUILD A STOVE! 19

CHAPTER 4
SLEEP SAFELY! 23

CHAPTER 5
MAKE AN ALARM! 27

DID YOU KNOW? 30

CONSIDER THIS! 31

LEARN MORE 31

GLOSSARY 32

INDEX 32

COULD YOU SURVIVE

A ZOMBIE APOCALYPSE?

THIS BOOK COULD SAVE YOUR LIFE!

Zombies are the living dead. They used to be humans. Then they died. But their bodies came back to life. An **apocalypse** is the destruction of the world. In a zombie apocalypse, zombies would overtake humans. They would destroy the world as we know it.

Zombies are no longer the people they were. They don't have free will. They can't think. They don't remember anything. On top of that, they stink! They have rotting skin. Their guts hang out. They limp. They move slowly. They're clumsy. They walk in a zigzag. They hang their heads. They moan. They groan. They're not smart. But they're focused. They destroy. They eat humans. And they especially love brains!

TIP Don't talk to zombies.
They can't understand you.

Zombies can be stronger than humans. They never get tired. They never sleep. They don't feel pain. They can hear well. They can smell well.

You may be able to kill 1 or 2 zombies. But you can't kill **hordes** of zombies. Hordes are large groups. Zombies attack as hordes. They close in on victims. They eat. They bite. By biting, they **infect** others. Infect means to make others sick. This is how zombies make more zombies.

One day, there could be more zombies than humans. Zombies would take over. Humans would become the food source. They'd be forced into hiding. This would lead to an apocalypse.

TIP Stay away from hordes especially when they're eating.

But you might be one of the lucky survivors. You have to be smart. First, know zombie weaknesses. Zombies are slow. They can't move well. They can't see well. They can't use tools. They can't heal. They can't grow. Second, know how to kill zombies. Cut off their heads. Or set them on fire.

Most importantly, know how to survive. Keep this in mind:

- You can only live 3 minutes without air.

- You can only live 3 days without water.

- You can only live 3 weeks without food.

This book offers you survival **hacks**, or tricks. Always be prepared. Good luck to you.

TIP Zombies follow noise.
Stay quiet!

SCIENCE CONNECTION

There's a sickness called the nodding disease. It mainly affects children ages 5 to 15. Victims of this sickness act like zombies. They nod a lot. They forget things. They light fires and wander off. They bite. Their bodies stop growing. Their muscles get weak. Their heads fall forward. Their brains are damaged. Many children have died. The exact number is not known. There is no cure. The nodding sickness first started in the 1960s. It started in areas away from big cities. It started in Sudan, Tanzania, and Uganda. These are all countries in Africa. Scientists are studying the sickness. They connected the sickness to a germ that is like a worm. This worm is carried by the black fly. Scientists think there could be other causes. One cause could be chemicals used in war. Another cause could be a lack of vitamin B.

CHAPTER 1

PROTECT YOUR BODY!

Oh no! Zombies are all around. Protect yourself. No part of your body is safe. So, wear **armor**. Armor is protective body covering. It's often used in wars. In a zombie apocalypse, you're at war with zombies. Prepare for battle!

TIP Wear a backpack. This will protect your back. It'll also hold your stuff.

HACK

1. Create the first layer. Wear a sweatshirt with a hood. Wear loose pants.

2. Create the second layer. Wear shoulder pads. Wear elbow pads. Wear arm pads. Wear a padded vest. Wear knee pads. Wear shin pads. Wear a **helmet**. Helmets are hard hats.

3. Create the top layer. Get **duct tape**. Duct tape is a strong tape. Tape everything together. Only wrap tape around 2 to 3 times. You want to be able to move.

4. Wear leather gloves. Wear **goggles**. Goggles protect the eyes.

TIP Wear a hat. Avoid sunburn. The sun can be just as dangerous as zombies.

explained by
STEM

The key to this hack is duct tape.

Duct tape is designed in a special way. It has 3 layers. The bottom is glue. The middle is cloth. The top is plastic. Duct tape is very sticky. It sticks to many different surfaces. It lasts a long time. It's **waterproof**. Waterproof means water can't get in. It stops leaks. Duct tape is very strong. It's made of **fibers**. Fibers are like little threads. They're woven into a crisscross pattern. This pattern lets the tape handle a lot of pressure. Duct tape is also flexible. It's not stiff. It can move. Most importantly, it keeps bites away from your skin!

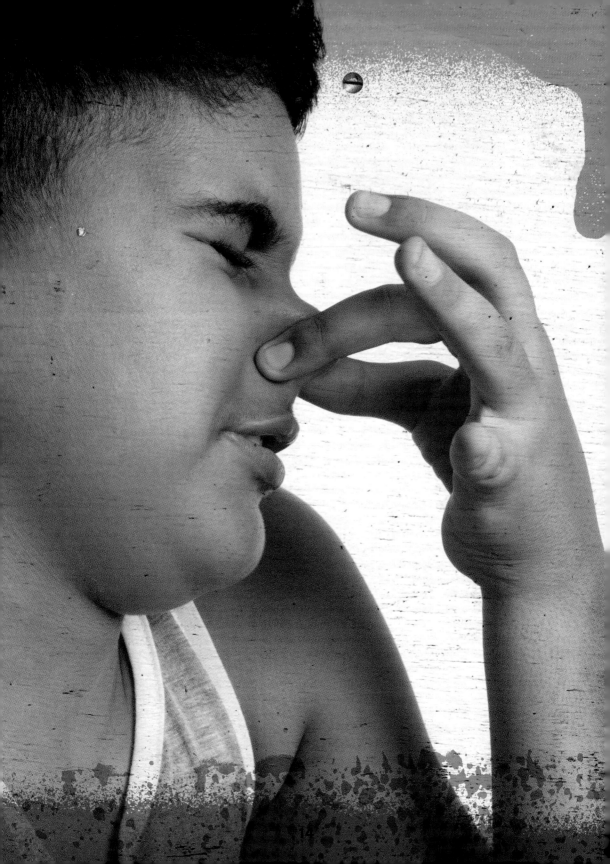

CHAPTER 2

HIDE YOUR SMELL!

Hide your human **scent** before heading out. Scent is smell. Zombies hear and smell you. That's how they find you. Get zombies off your trail. Make a stink bomb.

HACK

1. Get an empty soup can. Get an egg. Get milk. Get white vinegar. Get a plastic bag with a zipper.

2. Remove the top of the can.

3. Break an egg into the can.

4. Add milk and vinegar.

5. Put everything in a bag. Close it up tightly. Store it in a warm place. Place it in the sun.

6. Let it sit for a week. Let the stink build up.

7. Remove the bag when you're ready to use it.

TIP Toss the stink bomb in front of zombies. Then, run away.

STEM

The key to this hack is heat.

Heat changes the **chemistry** of milk and eggs. Chemistry means the makeup of things and how they change.

Heat spoils milk. Milk is mainly made of water and **lactose**. Lactose is milk sugar. Bad germs attack the lactose. They change milk. They sour milk. They make clumps. Yeasts and mold can grow. A smelly gas is released.

Heat also causes rotten eggs. It allows bad germs to grow. Eggs have **sulfides**. Sulfides are special minerals. When eggs rot, these sulfides are released. They make stinky gases. These gases deaden the sense of smell.

TIP Don't get any of the stink bomb on you.

17

There was a zombie chicken. His name was Miracle Mike. Mike was from Colorado. A farmer killed chickens for food. He cut off Mike's head. But Mike lived. This happened in 1945. The farmer only cut off the upper part of Mike's brain stem. Mike still had one ear. He still had most of his brain stem. This meant Mike's body still worked. Mike could walk. He could sit on a pole. He could crow a little bit. (His crowing sounded like a gurgling sound.) He could even eat. Food was injected into his stomach. Mike lived for 18 more months. The farmer took Mike on tour. He showed him off at circuses and other shows. Mike became famous. He was in magazines. He died on March 17, 1947. He died in a motel in Arizona. He choked in the middle of the night. A piece of corn got stuck in his throat.

CHAPTER 3

BUILD A STOVE!

You may need to cook food. A stove will help in other ways too. The stove can keep you warm. The smoke and fire keep zombies away.

TIP You can light crayons.
This will provide light for a little bit.

HACK

1. Get a tin coffee can. Empty it. Clean it.

2. Wear protective gloves. Use a can opener. Remove the bottom of the can.

3. Make air **vents**. Vents are holes. Make holes along the sides. Make holes along the top.

4. Get sticks and twigs. Push the sticks and twigs through the bottom of the can. Start a fire.

5. Put pots or pans on top.

TIP You can use potato chips to help start a fire.

STEM

The key to this hack is how its design moves heat.

Convection is heat transfer. It's the flow of heat. This stove uses convection. Hot air is blown around.

Fire needs air to burn. Air is pulled into the stove. It goes in the air vents. It moves up to the top. The metal reflects the heat back. The heat goes back into the fire. This allows the stove to make heat. The small space in the can keeps the heat in one place. This keeps the can nice and hot.

CHAPTER 4

SLEEP SAFELY!

Zombies never sleep. They can't see well at night. They're not as active. This gives you time to rest. Sleep gives you energy. But you still have to protect yourself. Zombies are still around. They can't swim. And there's a lake nearby. So, make a floating tent.

TIP You can also go high! Build a treehouse.

HACK

1. Get a lot of plastic water bottles. Make sure the bottles are empty. Make sure the lids are tightly in place.

2. Duct tape water bottles together. Make a flat bottom layer.

3. Layer rows of water bottles on top of each other. Duct tape everything together.

4. Put your tent on top of the **raft**. Rafts are flat floating structures.

5. Fix broken bottles. Cut out the damaged bottle. Duct tape a new bottle in its place.

TIP Don't forget oars or paddles.

STEM

The key to this hack is the plastic bottles.

These bottles are designed to be strong and **lightweight**. Lightweight means not heavy. The bottles are made of a special plastic. They take hundreds of years to break down.

Density measures how solid something is. All things are made of **molecules**. Molecules are very tiny. They're building blocks. In some things, molecules are close together. These things are dense. They sink. In other things, molecules are more spread out. There's more air. These things are less dense. They float. Plastic bottles float. They are less dense than water.

SPOTLIGHT BIOGRAPHY

Matt Mogk is a zombie expert. He's appeared on TV. He's also written books and articles. He knows about zombie science. He knows how to survive zombie attacks. He knows about zombie movies. He knows about zombie books. He wants to share his knowledge with others. He wants people to respect zombies. He created the Zombie Research Society (ZRS). He did this in 2007. The ZRS has over 100,000 members. Mogk thinks learning about zombies is important to humans' survival. He uses science when thinking about zombies. He said, "Zombies aren't around right now. But if one actually showed up on the front door, what would it look like? How would it function? How would its brain work? How would it hunt you? From there, we [come up with] survival strategies." Mogk was asked if he believed in a zombie apocalypse. He said, "It hasn't happened yet. But it could happen at any moment."

CHAPTER 5

MAKE AN ALARM!

Get a good night's sleep. Set traps. Set alarms. You want to know if zombies come. Make a **tripwire**. Tripwires are wires. They're stretched out close to the ground. They create a sound when touched. This will give you time to run away.

TIP You can also make ropes from plants.

HACK

1. Get a lot of plastic shopping bags.

2. Stretch out the bags. Tie them together.

3. Make several lines of bags. Then, braid them together. Make a strong rope.

4. Get things that make noise. Examples are spoons, bells, and tin cans.

5. Tie these things to the rope. Put them close enough together so they clink.

TIP You can use sounds to make zombies go to a specific place. You can set traps that way.

explained by
STEM

The key to this hack is the science of sound.

The tripwire creates sound. This sound alerts you to danger. Sound travels to the brain. First, sound waves reach the outer ear. Second, these waves move down the ear path to the eardrum. Third, they cause the eardrum to **vibrate**. Vibrate means to shake. Fourth, these vibrations move through 3 tiny ear bones. These ear bones are in the middle ear. This transfers the vibrations to the fluid in the inner ear. Fifth, the fluid vibrates hair cells. Sixth, these vibrations activate brain cells. The brain turns the vibrations into sounds.

DID YOU KNOW?

- Some people say zombies have a virus. A virus is like a bad germ. It makes people sick. It lives on living things. Zombies are dead. They're not alive. So, a zombie virus is impossible. A virus can't live on dead things. But there have been virus attacks. The "Hong Kong flu" happened in 1968. Flu is sickness caused by a virus. This flu killed between 1 and 4 million people.

- Researchers studied the safest places to avoid zombies. Australia is the safest area. It's surrounded by water on all sides. It also has the least amount of people per square mile. Canada is second. The United States is third. The ratings were based on location, land features, military and weapon access, and population size.

- The Centers for Disease Control and Prevention (CDC) protects people's health. Dave Daigle works for the CDC. He wanted to spread information about planning for disasters. But he knew people wouldn't read boring facts. So, he came up with a plan. He said, "I thought it would get more pickup if I used zombies." So, the CDC created a disaster plan for zombies. But it wasn't a real zombie guide. It gave general ideas for survival.

- Michigan State University has a class about zombies. The class is called "Surviving the Coming Zombie Apocalypse: Disasters, Catastrophes, and Human Behavior." It uses zombies to excite students. But the class is really about survival. Students are placed in groups. They have to work together. They practice survival skills.

- The Pentagon is made to survive a zombie apocalypse. It is home to the U.S. Department of Defense. It holds secret plans. It is protected against attacks of any kind. It even has a plan for zombie attacks. It was written as part of a training for young soldiers. The military thinks everyone should "always be prepared."

CONSIDER THIS!

TAKE A POSITION!

Do you have the right skills to survive a zombie apocalypse? Compare yourself to your family members. Who would be the best survivor? Argue your point with reasons and evidence.

SAY WHAT?

Read a fiction book about zombies. Or watch a movie about zombies. Explain what happened. Explain how zombies attacked. Explain how zombies changed people's lives. Explain how people died. Explain how people survived.

THINK ABOUT IT!

There are animals in nature that act like zombies. For example, there are horsehair worms. These worms attack crickets. They must get to water to have babies. So, they control crickets' minds. They make crickets move toward water. They make crickets jump in. Crickets drown themselves. Then, the horsehair worms come out. They make babies. They find their next victim. What other animals act like zombies?

LEARN MORE!

Dakota, Heather, and Ali Castro (illust.). *Zombie Apocalypse Survival Guide*. New York: Tangerine Press, 2013.

Loh-Hagan, Virginia. *Zombies*. Ann Arbor, MI: Cherry Lake Publishing, 2016.

Ogden, Charlie. *Surviving a Zombie Apocalypse*. New York, NY: Gareth Stevens Publishing, 2018.

Wacholtz, Anthony, and James Nathan (illust.). *Can You Survive a Zombie Apocalypse?* North Mankato, MN: Capstone Press, 2016.

GLOSSARY

apocalypse (uh-PAH-kuh-lips) the complete final destruction of the world

armor (AHR-mur) body covering used as protection

chemistry (KEM-ih-stree) the makeup of substances and how things change or act

convection (kuhn-VEK-shuhn) heat transfer

density (DEN-sih-tee) the measurement of how solid things are

duct tape (DUHKT TAYP) special tape that is strong, flexible, and waterproof

fibers (FYE-burz) little threads

goggles (GAH-guhlz) protective eyeglasses

hacks (HAKS) tricks

helmet (HEL-mit) hard covering for the head used for protection

hordes (HORDZ) large groups

infect (in-FEKT) to make others sick

lactose (LAK-tohs) milk sugar

lightweight (LITE-wayt) light to carry, not heavy

molecules (MAH-luh-kyoolz) the smallest particles of a substance

raft (RAFT) a flat, floating platform

scent (SENT) smell, odor

sulfides (SUL-fidez) special minerals

tripwire (TRIP-wire) a wire stretched close to the ground that works as a trap or alarm

vents (VENTS) airholes

vibrate (VYE-brayt) to move back and forth

waterproof (WAW-tur-proof) items that don't allow water to leak in

zombies (ZAHM-beez) undead creatures, corpses that comes back to life

INDEX

air, 21
alarm, 27–29
armor, 11–13

chemistry, 17
chicken, 18
convection, 21

density, 25
duct tape, 12, 13
ear, 29

fibers, 13

heat, 17, 21

lactose, 17

Mogk, Matt, 26
molecules, 25

nodding disease, 10

plastic bottles, 24, 25
sound waves, 29
stink bomb, 15–17
stove, 19–21
sulfides, 17
survival, 8, 30

tent, floating, 23–25
tripwire, 27–29

vibration, 29

waterproofing, 13

zombies, 4–9, 26, 30